BURIAL
OR
CREMATION?

What Does The Bible Say?

BURIAL
OR
CREMATION?
What Does The Bible Say?

Richard Cole Parke

Artos Publications™
P. O. Box 9801, McLean, VA 22102-0801
www.artospublications.com

BURIAL OR CREMATION? What Does The Bible Say?

Copyright © 2002 by *Artos Publications, LLC*

Library of Congress Control Number: 2002092713

ISBN 0-9721109-0-9

Please direct all correspondence to:

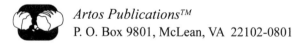 *Artos Publications*™
P. O. Box 9801, McLean, VA 22102-0801

www.artospublications.com

Layout design by Jill L. Redden
Printed in the United States of America

*To my parents and family
and to all whose love, prayers,
encouragement and support
made this book a reality.*

PREFACE

When my mother died in 1981 after a prolonged illness, her body was cremated in accordance with her personal wishes. For me, that event and decision raised some questions about death, burial and cremation, which motivated me to research and grapple with the very issues this book addresses. As a follower of Jesus Christ, I was curious to know what—if anything—the Bible might have to show me about these subjects.

For more than two decades, as a pastor, I've handled funerals, memorial services and interments for countless individuals of all ages and circumstances.

There were deaths of newborns, young children, young mothers, newly-weds, accidental deaths and deaths from long-term illness. I faced deaths resulting from AIDS and observed the heartaches that follow miscarriage, stillborn babies and SIDS (Sudden Infant Death Syndrome). Vividly I remember the memorial service for three people from the same family killed in a car wreck: a mother, her son and her grandson.

In every one of these heartrending situations, however, there was one common and urgent element:

The physical body of someone—a person whom someone else loved and valued—needed to be dealt with in a God-honoring manner.

My experience has shown that those facing the death of a loved one, in most cases, have never studied burial or cremation from a biblical, Christian perspective. Instead of seeking guidance from the Bible, family members make their decision on the basis of emotions, practicality, finances, legal directive of the deceased, environmental concerns or information from a funeral director. So what *does* the Bible say?

I have needed 20 years to process these highly emotional issues, but now I want to share the results of my study with others who might chance to be on that same journey seeking answers and guidance. That is how this book came to be. I trust it will be helpful to you.

Warmly and prayerfully,

Richard Cole Parke

INTRODUCTION

Burial? Cremation? Most people tend to avoid the subject of death because of the emotional stress associated with it. Nevertheless every one of us must face death at some time in the lives of family or friends, and—ultimately—we must face our own death.

The Bible tells us clearly that there is a time and a season for each one of us.

> . . . *a time to be born and a time to die, a time to plant and a time to uproot . . .*
> —Ecclesiastes 3:2

One day we must give account to our Creator.

> . . . *man is destined to die once, and after that to face judgment . . .*
> —Hebrews 9:27

Unpleasant and difficult as it may be—death is a topic we need to address. And after a death, one of the difficult issues we need to face is how to deal with the body of our loved one who has died.

BURIAL OR CREMATION?
What Does The Bible Say?

Perhaps you have lost a loved one. If the death is unexpected or sudden, you experience agony and trauma. You're in a daze. The telephone rings off the hook. You're unable to sleep. People need to be notified. Funeral preparations. Legal issues. Financial matters. Medical bills. Decisions—important ones—need to be made quickly, but you feel unready, adrift.

The purpose of this book is to discuss just one of these issues: *"How do we decide whether to bury or cremate the body of our loved one?"* This book will help you think through this decision before a death occurs.

Some people believe it doesn't matter at all what happens to their body after they die: *"I don't care what happens to my body. I'll be in heaven."* But such a perspective fails to take into account God's Word.

If we're followers of Jesus Christ and if our textbook is Scripture, then we should learn what it teaches. Wherever the Bible is clear,

1

we should obey if we desire to please God and experience His richest blessing. Surely God must have revealed to Adam and Eve the appropriate and acceptable manner of returning *"dust to dust."* And He *did*—in the Bible!

To lay the groundwork for this brief study about burial and cremation, we need to understand, first and foremost, that in spite of God's ongoing emphasis upon the development of our soul and spirit, God also gives special honor and dignity to the physical body.

God wants us to give special honor and dignity to our physical body while we are living.

1. We should honor our human body because of its heavenly origin.

. . . For you created my inmost being; you knit me together in my mother's womb. I praise you because I am fearfully and wonderfully made; your works are wonderful, I know that full well. My frame was not hidden from you when I was made in the secret place. When I was woven together in the depths of the earth, your

2

eyes saw my unformed body. All the days ordained for me were written in your book before one of them came to be.
—Psalm 139:13-16

He created it. It's His workmanship. He created not only my soul but also my *"frame."* Each member of my body functions according to His divine design.

. . . But in fact God has arranged the parts in the body, every one of them, just as he wanted them to be.
—1 Corinthians 12:18

2. **We should honor our human body because it's a "temple" of the Holy Spirit and houses our human spirit.**

. . . Do you not know that your body is a temple of the Holy Spirit, who is in you, whom you have received from God? You are not your own.
—1 Corinthians 6:19

The moment someone makes a conscious, volitional decision to commit himself to Jesus

3

Christ, the Spirit of God takes up residence in that person's body. The spiritual dimension is given new life—eternal life.

3. We should honor our human body because it is a vehicle or instrument of God.

> . . . *Do not offer the parts of your body to sin, as instruments of wickedness, but rather offer yourselves to God, as those who have been brought from death to life; and offer the parts of your body to him as instruments of righteousness.*
>
> —Romans 6:13

> . . . *you were bought at a price. Therefore honor God with your body.*
>
> —1 Corinthians 6:20

> . . . *Therefore, I urge you, brothers, in view of God's mercy, to offer your bodies as living sacrifices, holy and pleasing to God—this is your spiritual act of worship.*
>
> —Romans 12:1

God wants us to use our bodies to accomplish His righteous purposes and to please and glorify Himself.

4. We should honor our human body because our physical body is like a seed which gives promise of our future, heavenly resurrection body.

The Apostle Paul describes this concept,

> . . . *But God gives it [namely, the seed] a body as he has determined, and to each kind of seed he gives its own body.*
> . . . *So will it be with the resurrection of the dead. The body that is sown is perishable, it is raised imperishable; it is sown in dishonor, it is raised in glory; it is sown in weakness, it is raised in power; it is sown a natural body, it is raised a spiritual body.*
> . . . *And just as we have borne the likeness of the earthly man, so shall we bear the likeness of the man from heaven.*
> —1 Corinthians 15:38, 42-44, 49

If God wants us to give special honor and dignity to the physical body while we are alive, isn't it possible—even probable—that He would want us to do similarly after death? How did people in the Bible deal with the remains of their loved ones who died?

First, let's see what the Bible says about burial. Then we shall look at the topic of cremation.

BURIAL

Before starting, allow me to mention some of the pertinent vocabulary in the Bible! The Hebrew verb **qabar**—*"to inter"*—represents the act of placing a dead body into a grave or tomb. This word or its related derivatives—translated *"bury"* and *"burial"*—occur about 200 times in the Old Testament.

Similarly, in the New Testament—at least 50 times—the Greek words for *"grave,"* *"sepulcher"* and *"tomb"* all refer to a place of interment for a physical body. In fact, the more commonly-used words **mnema** and **mnemeion** come from the verb meaning *"to remember,"* hence they also carry with them the idea of being *"a place of remembrance"*—*"a memorial."*

1. God's people customarily buried their dead.

It was the Hebrews' custom to bury their dead. The followers of Jesus Christ prepared His body *"in accordance with Jewish burial customs."*

. . . Taking Jesus' body, the two of them wrapped it, with the spices, in strips of linen. This was **in accordance with Jewish burial customs.**

—John 19:40

When Moses died—as described in the Old Testament book of Deuteronomy—God could have dealt with Moses' body in any of a number of ways, but Scripture tells us that God chose burial.

Notice in the Scripture passage below the words in verse 6, *"He buried him . . ."*

. . . And Moses the servant of the LORD died there in Moab, as the LORD had said. **He buried him in Moab,** *in the valley opposite Beth Peor . . .*

—Deuteronomy 34:5-6a

Because Israel was God's chosen people, He instructed the Israelites to separate themselves from the heathen nations surrounding them in all aspects of life—and death. When we say that the Hebrews customarily buried their dead, we assume that what they buried was, in fact, the complete physical body of the person who died, not his ashes. Cremation was never a Jewish practice.

Jewish culture considered it a disgrace or a great misfortune to be deprived of burial.

> *A man may have a hundred children and live many years; yet no matter how long he lives, if he cannot enjoy his prosperity **and does not receive proper burial,** I say that a stillborn child is better off than he.*
> —Ecclesiastes 6:3

The prophet pronounced a curse against Queen Jezebel, King Ahab's wife, prophesying that she would die and her body would be deprived of burial.

> *". . . 'As for Jezebel, dogs will devour her on the plot of ground at Jezreel, **and no one will bury her.'** "*
> —2 Kings 9:10

Note the following examples from Scripture:

SARAH

Sarah was the wife of Abraham, the patriarch of Israel. It's most interesting—amazing really— that an entire chapter (Genesis 23) was devoted to Sarah's burial. Abraham went to extraordinary lengths to purchase a tomb for her, and Scripture mentions every detail—even the negotiations to purchase the cave of a man named Machpelah. The people of the land, the Hittites, told Abraham,

> "... *Bury your dead in the choicest of our tombs. None of us will refuse you his tomb for burying your dead.*"
> —Genesis 23:6

Then shortly thereafter we read the following,

> *Afterward Abraham buried his wife Sarah in the cave in the field of Machpelah near Mamre (which is at Hebron) in the land of Canaan. So the field and the cave in it were deeded to Abraham by the Hittites as a burial site.*
> —Genesis 23:19-20

ABRAHAM

Later, Abraham himself died and was buried alongside his wife Sarah. The funeral and burial were a rare opportunity for his family to come together in unity despite the earlier rivalry between his two sons, Isaac and Ishmael.

. . . *Altogether, Abraham lived a hundred and seventy-five years. Then Abraham breathed his last and died at a good old age, an old man and full of years; and he was gathered to his people.* **His sons Isaac and Ishmael buried him** *in the cave of Machpelah near Mamre, in the field of Ephron son of Zohar the Hittite, the field Abraham had bought from the Hittites.* **There Abraham was buried with his wife Sarah.** *After Abraham's death, God blessed his son Isaac, who then lived near Beer Lahai Roi.*

—Genesis 25:7-11

RACHEL

Rachel, you remember, was the favorite of Jacob's two wives. She died in childbirth. She

11

was the mother of Joseph and Benjamin.

> *. . . Then they moved on from Bethel. While they were still some distance from Ephrath, Rachel began to give birth and had great difficulty. And as she was having great difficulty in childbirth, the midwife said to her, "Don't be afraid, for you have another son." As she breathed her last—for she was dying—she named her son Ben-Oni. But his father named him Benjamin.* **So Rachel died and was buried** *on the way to Ephrath (that is, Bethlehem). Over her tomb Jacob set up a pillar, and to this day that pillar marks Rachel's tomb.*
>
> —Genesis 35:16-20

When Rachel died, Jacob set up a pillar because the Hebrew people considered all burial grounds sacred. They carefully marked the place where each body was buried. (See 1 Samuel 10:2)

ISAAC

As was the case with Isaac and Ishmael at Abraham's funeral, Isaac's funeral also gave opportunity to bring together Esau and Jacob to honor their father in burial. And remember, Esau and Jacob had experienced a very rocky, even hostile relationship for years. God often uses death to bring family members together.

> . . . *Jacob came home to his father Isaac in Mamre, near Kiriath Arba (that is, Hebron), where Abraham and Isaac had stayed. Isaac lived a hundred and eighty years. Then he breathed his last and died and was gathered to his people, old and full of years.* **And his sons Esau and Jacob buried him.**
> —Genesis 35:27-29

JACOB

As with the funerals of Abraham and Isaac, the funeral of Jacob now brought Joseph together at a stressful time with the very brothers who had betrayed him and sold him into slavery in Egypt in the first place! So God used the death and burial of their father Jacob not only to honor his life but also to bring about healing in their relationships with each other.

Jacob—whom God later renamed Israel—
actually died in Egypt prior to the Exodus.
Because Egyptians practiced embalming and
burial, his son Joseph very easily might have
buried him there in an Egyptian tomb.
Certainly it would have been less expensive and
more practical. However in Genesis, chapter
50, verses 1-14, the narrative tells us that
Joseph obeyed his father's request and—to
show him honor—expended unusual time and
effort to transport Jacob's body hundreds of
miles across the sandy desert in a huge caravan
of chariots and horsemen (Genesis 50:9). He
did all this so that he could bury his father in a
place of honor, in the family plot of his
forefathers, in the field of Machpelah, near
Mamre, in the land of Canaan.

*. . . When the time drew near for Israel to
die, he called for his son Joseph and said to
him, "If I have found favor in your eyes, put
your hand under my thigh and promise that
you will show me kindness and faithfulness.*
***Do not bury me in Egypt, but when I rest
with my fathers, carry me out of Egypt and
bury me where they are buried."***
—Genesis 47:29-30

Notice that all Pharaoh's officials accompanied Joseph. What an impression this must have made upon the Canaanites who lived in Canaan! Note the honor Joseph must have conveyed.

So Joseph went up to bury his father. All Pharaoh's officials accompanied him—the dignitaries of his court and all the dignitaries of Egypt . . . Chariots and horsemen also went up with him. It was a very large company . . . When the Canaanites who lived there saw the mourning at the threshing floor of Atad, they said, "The Egyptians are holding a solemn ceremony of mourning."

—Genesis 50:7, 9, 11

JOSEPH

In Genesis 50:22-26, Joseph gave explicit directions—commanded the children of Israel under oath—that even if he were to be embalmed and buried in Egypt, that one day they should carry his bones from Egypt to his final burial place with his forefathers in the land of Canaan. And more than 350 years later Moses sought to obey and honor Joseph's request and began this holy task. However, after 40 years of wandering in the wilderness, Moses died before entering the Promised Land. So actually it was Joshua's followers who completed the mission almost four centuries after Joseph's deathbed request!

> *. . . Moses took the bones of Joseph with him because Joseph had made the sons of Israel swear an oath. He had said, "God will surely come to your aid, and then you must carry my bones bones up with you from this place."*
>
> —Exodus 13:19

> *. . . And Joseph's bones, which the Israelites had brought up from Egypt, were buried at Shechem in the tract of land that Jacob bought for a hundred pieces of silver from the sons of Hamor, the father of Shechem. This became the inheritance of Joseph's descendants.*
>
> —Joshua 24:32

MOSES

The Bible describes Moses as *"the friend of God,"* yet when Moses disobeyed and dishonored God (Numbers 20:12), God disciplined him severely by not permitting him to enter Canaan—in life or in death—for *"He buried him in Moab."*

> *. . . And Moses the servant of the LORD died there in Moab, as the LORD had said.* **He buried him in Moab,** *in the valley opposite Beth Peor, but to this day no one knows where his grave is.*
>
> —Deuteronomy 34:5-6

Moses' burial was unique in two ways: (1) the LORD buried him. God honored Moses' life and service by personally attending to his burial. (2) The LORD kept Moses' grave in obscurity. We do not know exactly why God did this. God knows the tendency of the human heart to venerate—even worship—deceased national leaders or people of great significance to us in our lives. Perhaps God was precluding this from happening. He wanted the children of

Israel to focus only upon Him. (On this very matter see Matthew 17:1-8).

DAVID

Some consider David the greatest king of Israel, *"a man after God's own heart."* He was a shepherd, musician and poet as well as a king. Also he was an ancestor of Jesus Christ and chapter 11 of the New Testament book of Hebrews lists him as a hero of faith. After ruling Israel for 40 years, King David *"died and was buried."*

> *"Brothers, I can tell you confidently that the patriarch David died **and was buried**, and his tomb is here to this day."*
>
> —Acts 2:29

Again we read,

> *"For when David had served God's purpose in his own generation, he fell asleep; **he was buried** with his fathers **and his body decayed**."*
>
> —Acts 13:36

Notice that the Holy Spirit adds the phrase *"and his body decayed."*

Please hang onto this phrase because the Holy Spirit included it for a reason, namely, to show that burial of the entire body—not merely the ashes—is the example for God's people to follow. We shall discuss this phrase *"and his body decayed"* in more detail on pages 28-29.

JOHN THE BAPTIST

By retrieving his body and burying it, the disciples of John restored the honor and dignity that King Herod denied him by beheading him in prison (Mark 6:27).

> *John's disciples came and took his body **and buried it**.*
> —Matthew 14:12a

STEPHEN

When the Jewish leaders arrested Stephen and brought him before the Sanhedrin [the Jewish ruling council], he gave a powerful indictment

19

of the religious leaders, who in their fury stoned him to death. Such capital punishment was totally unjust and unusual in his case because Stephen had committed no capital crimes such as blasphemy (Leviticus 24:14, 16), spiritism (Leviticus 20:27), sexual offenses (Deuteronomy 22:21, 25), rebellion against parents (Deuteronomy 21:21) or disobeying the Sabbath (Numbers 15:35-36).

Because Stephen was innocent of these capital offenses, burial was a way—posthumously—of honoring his life, his faith and his testimony. Note how the Holy Spirit caused Luke, the author of the book of Acts, to select specifically the words *"godly men."*

> **Godly men buried** Stephen and mourned deeply for him.
>
> —Acts 8:2

Because Scripture is God-breathed (2 Timothy 3:16), God mentions even the slightest detail He feels is important for us to know!

God easily could have skipped the details of all these acts of burial, but the Holy Spirit chose to include them as examples for us to follow. God wants us to observe a pattern of how His people honored the bodies of these men and women of faith!

For everything that was written in the past was written to teach us, so that through endurance and the encouragement of the Scriptures we might have hope.
—Romans 15:4

God's people buried their dead. They even buried the disobedient.

In Deuteronomy we read,

*. . . If a man guilty of a capital offense is put to death and his body is hung on a tree, you must not leave his body on the tree overnight. **Be sure to bury him that same day**. . .*
—Deuteronomy 21:22-23

Similarly, in the case of Ananias and Sapphira, who lied to the Holy Spirit and whom God struck down in judgment, they were buried immediately. As is the case in many countries and situations where embalming is not practiced, burial took place within 24 hours. The entire account is recorded in Acts 5:1-10.

> *Then the young men came forward, wrapped up his body, and **carried him [Ananias] out and buried him** . . . At that moment she [Sapphira] fell down at his [Peter's] feet and died. Then the young men came in and, finding her dead, **carried her out and buried her beside her husband**.*
>
> —Acts 5:6, 10

In summary, Scripture makes clear—in the Old Testament and New Testament—that God's people buried their dead.

2. *Jesus believed in burial and expected the same for Himself.*

Whenever Jesus speaks or teaches on any subject, we should take special note.

In Matthew 8:21-22—in the context of teaching about the concept of discipleship—Jesus mentions burial as something very normal in the everyday world of the Jew. Luke 9:57-60 repeats the same incident.

Similarly, on another occasion Jesus tells the story of the rich man and the poor beggar named Lazarus—how each died and was buried.

*"The time came when the beggar died and the angels carried him to Abraham's side. The rich man also died **and was buried**."*
—Luke 16: 22

Later, the Apostle Matthew in Matthew 26:6-13 records how Mary of Bethany (See John 12:3) anointed Jesus' feet with expensive perfume and wiped them with her hair. Jesus explains that, when Mary poured this perfume on His body, she did it to prepare Him for burial. (Matthew 26:12)

That particular incident was so significant to Jesus' disciples that the gospel writers, Mark

23

and John, again make reference to it in Mark 14:8-9 and John 12:7.

3. The body of our Savior Jesus Christ was buried.

Isaiah the prophet prophesied this significant event—the burial of Christ—eight centuries before it happened!

And whenever God says He will do something, He always fulfills it!

> *"I foretold the former things long ago, my mouth announced them and I made them known; then suddenly I acted, and they came to pass."*
>
> —Isaiah 48:3

Isaiah prophesied that Jesus' body would be buried. In clear reference to the Messiah, he says,

> **He was assigned a grave** with the wicked, and with the rich in his death, though he had done no violence, nor was any deceit in his mouth.
>
> —Isaiah 53:9

The Hebrew word *qibrah*—translated *"grave"* here—literally means a *"sepulcher"* or *"burying place,"* which is exactly what happened to the body of Jesus Christ. A wealthy Jew named Joseph of Arimathea laid it in his own tomb.

Later, Joseph of Arimathea asked Pilate for the body of Jesus. Now Joseph was a disciple of Jesus, but secretly because he feared the Jews. With Pilate's permission, he came and took the body away. He was accompanied by Nicodemus, the man who earlier had visited Jesus at night. Nicodemus brought a mixture of myrrh and aloes, about seventy-five pounds. Taking Jesus' body, the two of them wrapped it, with the spices, in strips of linen. This was in accordance with Jewish burial customs. At the place where Jesus was crucified, there was a garden, and in the garden a new tomb, in which no one had ever been laid. Because it was the Jewish day of Preparation and since the tomb was nearby, they laid Jesus there.

—John 19:38-42

Jesus' disciples buried His body.

What greater example could we wish for? They carefully and tenderly prepared His body for burial according to Jewish custom.

The other gospel writers concur and recount this same information in Matthew 27:57-61, Mark 15:42-47 and Luke 23:50-56.

It is most significant to point out that the burial of Jesus is at the heart of the gospel message, for the Apostle Paul said,

> *For what I received I passed on to you as of first importance: that Christ died for our sins according to the Scriptures, **that he was buried** . . .*
>
> —1 Corinthians 15:3-4a

4. Burial best fits the concept of a future resurrection.

Old Testament Scripture lays the groundwork for linking physical burial and a future physical resurrection.

Job firmly believed that one day God would resurrect his body physically—the same body in which he died—and he would behold his Redeemer!

*I know that my Redeemer lives, and that in the end he will stand upon the earth. And after my skin has been destroyed, **yet in my flesh I will see God**; I myself will see him with my own eyes—I, and not another. How my heart yearns within me!*

—Job 19:25-27

In the Old Testament God's people strongly believed in a future resurrection.

Abraham, the Old Testament patriarch, believed that even if he had slain Isaac on the altar at Mount Moriah, God could have and would have raised Isaac from the dead.

*He said to his servants, "Stay here with the donkey while I and the boy go over there. We will worship and then **we** will come back to you."*

—Genesis 22:5

27

One thousand years before Christ, King David foretold Jesus' death and resurrection. The language of his statement shows that he anticipated burial, not cremation.

> . . . because you will not abandon me to the grave, nor will you let your Holy One [the Messiah, Jesus Christ] see **decay**.
>
> —Psalm 16:10

The word *"decay"* here in the Old Testament is a somewhat general term, but in the New Testament, the Apostle Peter refers to the same prophecy of King David and—guided by the Holy Spirit—clarifies exactly what God meant.

> *Seeing what was ahead, he [King David] spoke of the resurrection of the Christ, that* ***he was not abandoned to the grave, nor did his body see decay.***
>
> —Acts 2:31

The Greek word **diaphthora** leaves no doubt. **Diaphthora** describes the normal, natural process of physical decomposition and decay, which could only happen as the result of burial. Specifically, it means *"to rot thoroughly."*

This word appears six times in the New Testament—one time referring to King David whose body *did* experience decay—and five times referring to Jesus Christ whose physical body *did not* experience decay. Peter is saying that the body of Jesus was not subject to the process of decay because Jesus' body would be resurrected! The Jewish readers clearly understood that Peter was describing burial.

The same Greek word **diaphthora** also appears in Acts 13:36, a Scripture quoted on page 18 where the Apostle Paul makes this same point about the natural process of decay.

Elsewhere—in another passage—King David also strongly affirmed his faith in a future physical resurrection shortly after his and Bathsheba's infant son died. Although King David mourned while his newborn son was lying sick, when the baby did die—and was buried according to custom [not specifically mentioned but assumed]—David expressed his strong belief that he would see his son again one day in the future when he said,

"But now that he is dead, why should I fast? Can I bring him back again? **I will go to him** *[i.e. at the future resurrection of all believers], but he will not return to me."*
—2 Samuel 12:23

New Testament Scripture welds together these same two concepts: (1) death and burial of the physical body, and (2) a future physical resurrection—particularly its analogy and symbolism in the ordinance of baptism. Baptism was not only a public proclamation of faith but also a public *"burial"* in water.

The Apostle Paul explains that baptism (which means *"immersion"*) symbolizes death and burial of the *"old self"*—that is, the person's life prior to making a commitment to Jesus Christ (Ephesians 4:22). For this reason the person being baptized is lowered completely beneath the water symbolizing his identification with the death and burial of Jesus Christ.

Likewise, as the person being baptized comes up from beneath the water, it is a beautiful

picture of the believer's new spiritual nature—
his *"new self"* (Ephesians 4:24)—and his
identification with Jesus' resurrection.

> *Or don't you know that all of us who were*
> *baptized into Christ Jesus were baptized*
> *into his death? We were therefore buried*
> *with him through baptism into death in*
> *order that, just as Christ was raised from*
> *the dead through the glory of the Father, we*
> *too may live a new life.*
> —Romans 6:3-4

Baptism symbolizes the spiritual birth or
transaction that already has taken place in a
person's heart (See Acts 16:31-33). So when a
believer in Jesus Christ is baptized, he is telling
others publicly of his new allegiance and new
spiritual life within. At the same time,
however, he is also affirming Christ's
resurrection and his own future resurrection.

> *. . . having been **buried with him in baptism***
> ***and raised with him** through your faith in*
> *the power of God, who raised him from the*
> *dead.*
> —Colossians 2:12

31

Indeed a physical burial and a physical resurrection were the very heart of the message of the Early Church! The Apostle Paul links them together inextricably when he says,

> *For what I received I passed on to you as of first importance: that Christ died for our sins according to the Scriptures, **that he was buried, that he was raised on the third day** according to the Scriptures.*
>
> —1 Corinthians 15:3-4

And, furthermore—as far as tying together a physical burial and a physical resurrection—the Apostle Paul makes very clear that a person's physical body is to be buried.

> *. . . So will it be with the resurrection of the dead. The **body** that is sown [namely, in the ground] is perishable, it is raised imperishable; it is sown in dishonor, it is raised in glory; it is sown in weakness, it is raised in power; it is sown a **natural body**, it is raised a **spiritual body**.*
>
> —1 Corinthians 15:42-44

For God's people—burial has always been a public testimony of one's faith and one's assurance of a future physical resurrection.

CREMATION

The English words *"cremation"* and *"cremate"* are transliterations of the Latin infinitive *cremare* meaning *"to burn"* and its past participle *crematus*, "having been burned." Specifically, therefore, cremation refers to the act or the process of burning a dead body.

Cremation is quick, sanitary, less expensive than burial, and practical for purposes of transporting the remains of a loved one from one place to another.

All these arguments in favor of cremation are undeniably true, but as with the case for burial, ultimately the Bible must be the source of truth and the guide for living for every follower of Christ. Therefore one ought to ask, *"How does cremation line up with Scripture?"*

No doubt about it, God is more than able to raise up from ashes the bodies of believers and unbelievers alike—whether such a condition resulted from intentional cremation or was the consequence of a natural fire, explosion or bomb blast.

But as with other life issues and questions, we need to look at cremation carefully in light of Scripture: *"What is God's way for handling the usual circumstances of death?"*

At the beginning of this book I explained how my mother's cremation had stimulated my curiosity, raised some questions, and set me on this long, two-year journey through the Bible to find answers. My search was never tedious, dull or even morbid. I learned some fascinating things along the way. And what I discovered—as well as what I did not discover—helped me immensely.

Again, as I did with regard to the topic of burial —to be fair and equal—I also searched the Bible cover to cover for references to cremation. I spared no effort in looking up key words such as *"ashes"* and *"burn"* to point me to answers to my questions—not knowing exactly what I might uncover in the process.

USES OF THE TERM "ASHES" IN THE BIBLE

The English word translated *"ashes"* occurs 39 times in the Old Testament and four times in the New Testament. In the Old Testament, twenty-five times—in a context of mourning and repentance—*"ashes"* refer to a powdery substance from a furnace, which can be blown about by the wind. Ten times it refers specifically to the residue from burnt animal sacrifices. Twice the word refers, generically, to ashes strewn about—no further detail—and twice it refers to pulverized clay or earth, hence dust.

In Genesis 18:27 there is a play on words between *"dust"* (Hebrew **aphar**) and *"ashes"* (Hebrew **epher**), which together symbolize the lowliness and frailty of human life.

Then Abraham spoke up once again: "Now that I have been so bold as to speak to the LORD, ***though I am nothing but dust and ashes. . ."***

—Genesis 18:27

In the New Testament passages, Matthew 11:21 and Luke 10:13, a Greek word—of uncertain origin—translated *"ashes"* occurs in a context of repentance, namely, the phrase *"sackcloth and ashes."* In Hebrews 9:13, again this same word occurs in a context of religious animal sacrifice. The last occurrence of *"ashes"* in the New Testament—in 2 Peter 2:6—involves a verb which means specifically *"to incinerate"* and refers to Sodom and Gomorrah, which God condemned *"by burning them to ashes."*

Next I looked at instances and examples of *"burning"* mentioned in the Bible—some positive in nature, others negative. These appeared to have nothing to do with cremation, yet I studied them for whatever light they might bring to bear on the topic.

SOME POSITIVE EXAMPLES OF "BURNING" IN THE BIBLE

1. Burning of aromatic spices in honor of the deceased.

Three times in the Old Testament the Hebrew word for *"burning"* refers to the *"burning"* of aromatic spices in honor of the deceased kings of Judah and Israel. These burnings, however, were not cremation. (See 2 Chronicles 16:14; 2 Chronicles 21:19; Jeremiah 34:5)

2. *Burnt offerings and sacrifices to Yahweh, the God of Israel*

In the Torah, the five books of Moses—Genesis, Exodus, Leviticus, Numbers and Deuteronomy—God gave clear directions as to *how, where, why* and *what* to sacrifice. God was very specific. And when God's people obeyed Him, it always pleased Him.

SOME NEGATIVE EXAMPLES OF "BURNING" IN THE BIBLE

1. *Human child sacrifices to Molech*

Throughout the Old Testament God commanded that only certain specific, unblemished animals be burned as sacrifices—never a human. This was strictly forbidden.

" 'Do not give any of your children to be sacrificed to Molech, for you must not profane the name of your God. I am the LORD.' "

—Leviticus 18:21

But despite God's clear commandments, the children of Israel disobeyed. Instead of the burnt offerings and sacrifices prescribed in the Mosaic Law, they perverted God's commandment by causing their children to *"pass through the fire"* sacrificing them to the heathen God Molech.

You must not worship the LORD *your God in their way, because in worshiping their gods, they do all kinds of detestable things the* LORD *hates.* **They even burn their sons and daughters in the fire as sacrifices to their gods.**

—Deuteronomy 12:31

Scripture mentions this same heathen practice and condemns it in 2 Kings 17:17, Jeremiah 19:5, Ezekiel 16:21 and Psalm 106:37-38.

- It was strictly forbidden. (Leviticus 18:21, Jeremiah 19:5)
- God hated it. (Deuteronomy 12:31)
- It profaned God's name. (Leviticus 18:21, 20:3)
- It provoked God's anger. (2 Kings 17:17-18)
- It was an abominable, detestable act. (Deuteronomy 12:31)
- It was punishable by death. (Leviticus 20:2)

Of course, this detestable heathen practice had no relation to cremation as we know it, because these sacrifices to Molech involved living human children.

2. Direct divine judgment by fire of living persons

These instances were not cremation either, but in my search through the Bible I was leaving no stone unturned.

Interestingly enough, I discovered from my study that many instances of burning were acts of God's judgment—destruction of people and things that were an abomination to Him. I noted, however, that the persons God judged were burned while they were alive—*not after death.*

They were acts of divine displeasure and judgment—and, as far as dealing with the dead, they were exceptions to customary burial and were *not the norm* for God's people.

Such direct divine judgment by fire specifically addressed sins of a sexual nature: immorality, perversions, incest and prostitution.

• Gross immorality and sexual perversions

God destroyed Sodom and Gomorrah by fire for these very reasons:

Now the men of Sodom were wicked and were sinning greatly against the LORD.
—Genesis 13:13

*Then the L*ORD *said, "The outcry against Sodom and Gomorrah is so great and their sin is so grievous . . ."*

—Genesis 18:20

In a similar way, Sodom and Gomorrah and the surrounding towns gave themselves up to sexual immorality and perversion.

—Jude 7a

And so God destroyed them all by fire—as an act of divine judgment:

Then the LORD rained down burning sulphur *on Sodom and Gomorrah—from the L*ORD *out of the heavens. Thus he overthrew those cities and the entire plain, including all those living in the cities—and also the vegetation in the land.*

—Genesis 19:24-25

. . . if he condemned the cities of Sodom and Gomorrah **by burning them to ashes**, *and made them an example of what is going to happen to the ungodly. . .*

—2 Peter 2:6

God was no more lenient with the sins of incest or prostitution.

- Incest

*" 'If a man marries both a woman and her mother, it is wicked. Both he and **they must be burned in the fire**, so that no wickedness will be among you.' "*

—Leviticus 20:14

- Prostitution

*About three months later Judah was told, "Your daughter-in-law Tamar is guilty of prostitution, and as a result she is now pregnant." Judah said, "Bring her out and **have her burned to death!**"*

—Genesis 38:24

*" 'If a priest's daughter defiles herself by becoming a prostitute, she disgraces her father; **she must be burned in the fire**.' "*

—Leviticus 21:9

God not only dealt severely with sexual sin, but also with outright rebellion and perversions of a spiritual nature.

- Spiritual perversions and disobedience

Aaron's sons Nadab and Abihu took their censers, put fire in them and added incense; and they offered unauthorized fire before the LORD, contrary to his command. **So fire came out from the presence of the LORD and consumed them,** *and they died before the LORD.*

—Leviticus 10:1-2

3. Indirect divine judgment by death, then fire

In this one instance, cited from the book of Joshua in the Old Testament, God first commanded Achan's death, then afterwards his body was burned. In fact, God was so angry at Achan's sin that his family suffered the same fate. God made an example of them all!

You might ask, *"What in the world was Achan's big sin?"* The Bible tells us.

During the assault on the city of Jericho, Achan had been guilty of violating God's covenant when he stole forbidden booty and hid it in his tent in direct disobedience of God's express command.

The LORD said to Joshua, "Stand up! What are you doing down on your face? Israel has sinned; they have violated my covenant, which I commanded them to keep. They have taken some of the devoted things; they have stolen, they have lied, they have put them with their own possessions." . . .
" 'He who is caught with the devoted things shall be destroyed by fire, along with all that belongs to him. He has violated the covenant of the LORD and has done a disgraceful thing in Israel!' " . . .
Then all Israel stoned him, and after they had stoned the rest [of Achan's family], they burned them.
—Joshua 7:10-11, 15, 25b

Each of these situations of divine judgment described above, however, were exceptions—not the rule, not the norm for God's people. Their general custom was to bury the dead.

Other than these cases of God's divine judgment by fire, *in no instance except one*, were the bodies of deceased Israelites burned.

4. *The burning of the bodies of King Saul and his sons*

King Saul and his sons are the best-known exceptions to the normal burial procedures described in the Bible.

In those extraordinary circumstances following the battle on Mount Gilboa, the Philistines had hung the bodies of King Saul and his sons on the wall of the open square of Beth Shan and had beheaded and mutilated them.

At peril to their own lives, the men of Jabesh Gilead marched all night to retrieve the bodies of King Saul and his sons, then—to prevent any additional abuse and desecration by the Philistines—burned them at Jabesh, but such burning was restricted to skin and flesh and did *not* destroy their bones, which they took and buried.

*When the people of Jabesh Gilead heard of what the Philistines had done to Saul, all their valiant men journeyed through the night to Beth Shan. They took down the bodies of Saul and his sons from the wall of Beth Shan and went to Jabesh, **where they burned them. Then they took their bones and buried them** under a tamarisk tree at Jabesh and they fasted seven days.*

—1 Samuel 31:11-13

By the way, this mention of fasting is not a trivial or superfluous detail here. God included these words in the Bible for a reason. The words *"and they fasted seven days"* shows to what lengths the men of Jabesh Gilead were willing to go in order to honor the bodies of King Saul and his sons.

Later King David commended the men of Jabesh Gilead for burying Saul (2 Samuel 2:4-5) and removed the bones of Saul and Jonathan from that first burial site in Jabesh and *reburied* them in the family tomb of Saul's father, Kish, in Zela—one of the cities in the territory belonging to the tribe of Benjamin. (2 Samuel 21:12-14)

48

5. *Burning connected to warfare*

Not surprisingly, some instances of *"burning"* in Scripture were connected to warfare—for example, these from the Old Testament book of Joshua:

> *Then they burned the whole city and everything in it, but they put the silver and gold and the articles of bronze and iron into the treasury of the LORD's house.*
>
> —Joshua 6:24

> *So Joshua burned Ai and made it a permanent heap of ruins, a desolate place to this day.*
>
> —Joshua 8:28

> *Everyone in it they put to the sword. They totally destroyed them, not sparing anything that breathed, and he burned up Hazor itself.*
>
> —Joshua 11:11

But because these instances of *"burning"* occurred in the context of military warfare, of course, they were not equivalent to the modern practice of cremation. Cremation, as we know it, is a decision—by free will—to burn a deceased person's body.

6. Burning connected to God's future judgment

Another instance of *"burning"* in Scripture —although clearly not related to cremation—is definitely worth mentioning.

Perhaps the most significant instance of *"burning"* actually will occur far in the future —at God's day of judgment, at the *"great white throne"* which the Apostle John mentions in Revelation 20:11.

The Apostle Peter describes this fiery judgment as follows,

> *By the same word the present heavens and earth are **reserved for fire**, being kept for the day of judgment and destruction of ungodly men.*
>
> —2 Peter 3:7

Ultimately, Satan, the beast and the false prophet, and all who have rejected God's Son, will be condemned to eternal fire—in hell.

John the Apostle writes in the book of Revelation,

> *And the devil, who deceived them, was thrown into* **the lake of burning sulfur,** *where the beast and the false prophet had been thrown. They will be tormented day and night for ever and ever . . . If anyone's name was not found written in the book of life, he was thrown into* **the lake of fire.**
> —Revelation 20:10, 15

7. *God's disapproval and curse upon the Moabites*

The clearest and most relevant reference to cremation occurs in the Old Testament book of Amos.

In this particular case the Moabites had *"burned"* the bones of the king of Edom. Was this cremation, as we know it? We cannot be

51

absolutely certain because the context provides no additional information, but Scripture does tell us that God disapproved and, in fact, He cursed the Moabites for what they had done.

*This is what the LORD says: "For three sins of Moab, even for four, I will not turn back my wrath. **Because he burned, as if to lime, the bones of Edom's king,** I will send fire upon Moab . . ."*

—Amos 2:1-2a

In this section on cremation—just as I did with the topic of burial—I simply went to the Bible to find out what it had to say. My original question was, *"How does cremation line up with Scripture?"*—And, as best I can, I've tried to present the information I uncovered, so that you can think about it and draw your own conclusion.

SUMMARY

Having looked to see what the Bible has to say—first about burial, then cremation—I think now it's appropriate to wrap things up.

BURIAL

In addition to God's ongoing emphasis on the development of our soul and spirit, the Bible clearly teaches:

- God created the human body.
- God gave it great honor and dignity.
- God, therefore, expects us to treat it with respect and care, in life—and in death.

The Bible gives many examples of burial and clear reasons for it:

1. Burial was customary among God's people both before and after Jesus Christ.

2. Jesus not only believed in burial of the dead but also expected the same for Himself.

3. The body of our Savior was buried. This is of paramount importance because we want to follow His example.

4. Burial best fits the biblical concept of a future resurrection.

CREMATION

From the Bible I discovered the following:

1. Wherever Scripture mentions *"ashes,"* either it refers primarily to acts of mourning or repentance or—in other contexts—to the burned remains of religious animal sacrifices.

2. Some Scriptural examples of *"burning"* are positive such as burning aromatic spices in honor of the deceased or presenting burnt offerings and sacrifices that God commanded and approved.

3. Other examples are negative—associated with heathen practices, associated with sin and divine judgment or associated with warfare.

4. Those references to *"burning,"* which I cited, have no relation to the practice of cremation—ancient or modern.

5. The instance where the men of Jabesh Gilead burned the bodies of King Saul and his son Jonathan was only to prevent further mutilation and desecration, but their bones were buried.

6. In the one place perhaps where Scripture does appear to address cremation as we know it (Amos 2:1-2a) the context mentions Israel's heathen neighbor Moab, but God curses the Moabites for their action.

APPLICATION

At the start of this book we acknowledged that death is an uncomfortable thought for most, not to mention how we deal with the body of our loved one. But no doubt about it, these topics—burial and cremation—are indeed relevant, and more so as we grow older.

In this specific context, I make the simple assumption that each of us wants to honor not only our loved one but also God to whom one day we will give account.

> *So then, each of us will give an account of himself to God.*
> —Romans 14:12

Ultimately, how we deal with the body of our loved one is a matter of conscience, of course. In making the decision, however, it is always wise to search the Scriptures and to take into account what God has revealed in the Bible—especially where it speaks clearly.

As a Christian, I've discovered two helpful guidelines when facing life issues or decisions:

- Where the Bible speaks clearly, obey it!

- Where the Bible is silent, God gives a person freedom within the parameters of other biblical truths and principles.

OTHER MATTERS

Someone might ask,
"What if a loved one, who has already died, has made a specific request to be cremated— either verbally or in a legal document?"

Suppose *you* have the responsibility to make decisions about the body of your loved one. After reading this book, suppose you change your mind about burial and cremation. Suppose you're torn emotionally—you wish to respect the wishes of the deceased, but at the same time you hold a different view. What should you do?

There are no pat answers to these difficult questions. Jesus did say that this issue—dealing with the dead—although important as far as earthly matters, of course, is really secondary to being His disciple,

> *But Jesus told him, "Follow me, and let the dead bury their own dead."*
> —Matthew 8:22

Our primary mission is to follow Him. To follow Jesus means showing His love and care for people—people who need God's healing and comfort, people who tend to wander like sheep, people who get *"lost"* spiritually.

Therefore, at a time of sorrow our focus should be upon the loved ones whom the deceased has left behind. This is not the time to discuss fine points of theology. It's best to think through and make such decisions *before* a death, not afterwards.

Rather, we need to ask ourselves how our decisions and our actions can best communicate Jesus' message and show His love and compassion to family and friends who are brokenhearted and hurting.

If you are a follower of Jesus, ask God for sensitivity and wisdom. He promises to give it to you.

If any of you lacks wisdom, he should ask God, who gives generously to all without finding fault, and it will be given to him.
—James 1:5

God also promises to give you peace about such matters,

> *Do not be anxious about anything, but in everything, by prayer and petition, with thanksgiving, present your requests to God. And the peace of God, which transcends all understanding, will guard your hearts and your minds in Christ Jesus.*
>
> —Philippians 4:6-7

POSTSCRIPT

If you have received this book at a time of illness, crisis or loss, my sincere sympathy goes out to you. May God guide you in the decisions you make during this difficult time. May *"the Father of compassion and the God of all comfort"* console and comfort you.

Also, if you are unsure and want to be certain about going to heaven, please write and request a *free* booklet entitled ***How to Have a Happy and Meaningful Life***. This booklet explains how to establish a personal relationship with God and experience His wonderful plan for your life—now and in eternity.

To receive your free copy, please send a stamped, self-addressed envelope to:

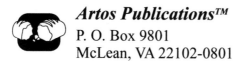

Artos Publications™
P. O. Box 9801
McLean, VA 22102-0801

YOUR COMMENTS

This is the first edition. Therefore, if you notice a misspelling or other error, please bring it to my attention. Also, I welcome your suggestions, criticisms and comments. I'll receive them gratefully and thoughtfully even if I may not be able to acknowledge personal correspondence.

Richard Cole Parke

ABOUT THE AUTHOR

Richard Parke made a personal commitment to Jesus Christ in 1964 as a student at the University of California, Riverside. He began full-time Christian ministry in 1966 and was ordained as a minister ten years later. After several years in Greece as a missionary, he became an associate pastor at McLean Bible Church, McLean, Virginia, in 1982. Currently he resides in Annandale, Virginia.

ORDER FORM

TO ORDER
Make check payable to:
Artos Publications™
P. O. Box 9801, McLean, VA 22102-0801
Toll Free Telephone: (888) 281-5170
COMMENTS AND INQUIRIES
rparke@artospublications.com or www.artospublications.com

Pricing *(for individuals only)*

1-9 books ....$7.99 each
10-99 books ....$6.99 each
100+ books ....$5.99 each

Quantity	**Subtotal** ....
4.5% Sales tax for Virginia residents only	**Subtotal** ....

*(Multiply **Pricing** subtotal above by .045.)*

Shipping & Handling *(for individuals only)*

Orders under $10.00..$3.50
$10.00 - $19.99...$4.00
$20.00 - $29.99...$4.50
$30.00 - $49.99...$5.00
$50.00 - $99.99...$6.00
$100.00+...6% of **Pricing Subtotal**

Subtotal...................

Total...................

*If you cannot find this book, or it is not available
at your local bookstore, please see the ordering information above.
Bookstores: Standard terms apply. Net 30.*

SHIPPING INFORMATION
Please print clearly

Name..
Organization...
Address...Apt.#.................
City..State........Zip...................
Phone...Fax..............................